Stuarts

Dr. Anne Millard

Evans Brothers Limited

Published in this edition 2009 by
Evans Brothers Ltd
2A Portman Mansions
Chiltern St
London W1U 6NR

Printed in Hong Kong

A catalogue record for this book is available from the British
Library.

ISBN 978 0 237 53853 8

Acknowledgements

Series Editor – Su Swallow
Editor – Jill A. Laidlaw
Designer – Ann Samuel
Production – Jenny Mulvanny
Maps and illustrations – Nick Hawken and Mike White

For permission to reproduce copyright material, the author and publishers gratefully acknowledge the following:

Cover (main) Bridgeman Art Library, (background) Bridgeman Art Library/Museum of Fine Art, Budapest, (top) Mary Evans Picture Library, (middle) /Bridgeman Art Library/Royal College of Physicians, London, (bottom) e.t. archive, London **Title page** Mary Evans Picture Library, London. **Pages 6** (top) Robert Harding Picture Library, London/Marquess of Salisbury, (bottom) English Heritage, Chiswick House, London. **Page 7** (top) Bridgeman Art Library, London, (bottom) Mary Evans Picture Library, London. **Page 8** (top) Mary Evans Picture Library, London, (bottom) Bridgeman Art Library/Chateau de Versailles. France. **Page 9** (top and bottom) Robert Harding Picture Library, London. **Page 10** (top) Bridgeman Art Library, London, (bottom) Bridgeman Art Library, London/Museum of London. **Page 11** Bridgeman Art Library/ The Victoria and Albert Museum, London. **Page 12** (top) Robert Harding Picture Library, London (bottom) e.t. archive, London/Stoke Museum. **Page 13** Robert Harding, London/Marquess of Anglesey. **Page 14** Mary Evans Picture Library, London. **Page 15** (top) Mary Evans Picture Library, London, (bottom) e.t. archive, London. **Page 16** Mary Evans Picture Library, London. **Page 17** (top and bottom) Mary Evans Picture Library, London. **Page 18** British Museum/Bridgeman Art Library, London. **Page 19** (top) Robert Harding Picture Library, London, (bottom) Museum of Fine Arts, Budapest/Bridgeman Art Library, London. **Page 20** (top) Robert Harding Picture Library, London, (bottom) The Victoria and Albert Museum/The Bridgeman Art Library, London. **Page 21** (top) Mary Evans Picture Library, London, (bottom) e.t. archive, London. **Page 22** (top) e.t. archive, London, (middle) Robert Harding Picture Library, London, (bottom) e.t. archive, London. **Page 24** National Maritime Museum, London/e.t. archive, London. **Page 25** (left) Mary Evans Picture Library, London, (right) Robert Harding Picture Library. **Page 26** (top and bottom) e.t. archive, London. **Page 27** (top) Brideman Art Library, London/Ham House, Surrey, (bottom) Bruce Coleman Limited. **Page 28** (top) e.t. archive, London, (bottom) e.t. archive/Royal Society. **Page 29** Brideman Art Library/Royal College of Physicians, London, (bottom) Mary Evans Picture Library, London.

Stuarts

1567	Mary Queen of Scots abdicates and her son becomes James VI of Scotland
1603	James inherits Elizabeth I of England's throne and becomes James I of England, Scotland, Ireland and Wales
1605	The Gunpowder Plot
1607	Foundation of Jamestown, Virginia, North America
1610	Discovery of Hudson Bay
1611	Publication of the King James Bible
1616	Death of William Shakespeare
1620	Pilgrim Fathers sail for North America in the *Mayflower*
1624-30	War with Spain
1627-9	War with France
1628	The Petition of Right Harvey discovers the circulation of the blood
1629-40	Charles I rules without Parliament
1638	The National Covenant
1641	The Grand Remonstrance
1642-5	Civil War
1648	Pride's Purge
1649	Execution of Charles I
1650	Cromwell fights in Ireland
1651	Navigation Act
1652-4	War against the Dutch
1656-9	War against Spain
1658	Death of Oliver Cromwell
1660	Restoration of Charles II
1660-65	The Clarendon Code
1660-69	Samuel Pepys keeps his diary
1665-7	War against the Dutch
1665	The plague
1666	The Great Fire of London
1672-4	War against the Dutch
1685	Death of Charles II, James II comes to the throne
1688	James II thrown out of England The Glorious Revolution William and Mary rule
1689-97	War against France
1690	Battle of the Boyne
1702	William dies, Anne comes to the throne
1702-13	War of the Spanish Succession
1707	The Act of Union
1714	Hanoverian rule begins

Contents

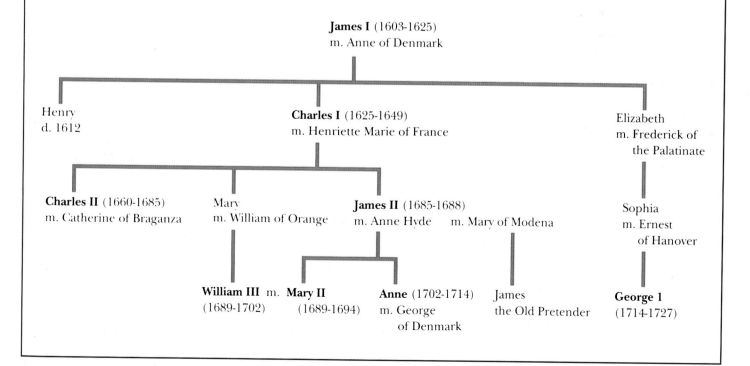

James I (1603-1625)
m. Anne of Denmark

Henry
d. 1612

Charles I (1625-1649)
m. Henriette Marie of France

Elizabeth
m. Frederick of
the Palatinate

Charles II (1660-1685)
m. Catherine of Braganza

Mary
m. William of Orange

James II (1685-1688)
m. Anne Hyde   m. Mary of Modena

Sophia
m. Ernest
of Hanover

William III m. **Mary II**
(1689-1702)   (1689-1694)

Anne (1702-1714)
m. George
of Denmark

James
the Old Pretender

George 1
(1714-1727)

James 1 and Charles 1

James I (c.1623) standing next to the crown that was melted down by Parliament during the Commonwealth (see pages 8-9).

James I (1566-1625)

In 1567 Mary, Queen of Scots (1542-87), abdicated and fled to England. Her 13 month-old son became James VI of Scotland. He had a miserable, lonely childhood, but he was clever and well educated. On 24 March 1603, messengers rode north from London to tell James that his mother's cousin, Queen Elizabeth I (1533-1603), was dead and that he was now King James I of England, Wales and Ireland.

James came to England at a very difficult time. The king had to 'live off his own', that is, off the money he got from his lands and from customs duties (taxes paid on goods brought into the country). With this money he had to pay all the costs of running the government and the court. But prices were rising, foreign wars were very expensive and the government was playing a more active part in ruling the country, so the monarch was often very short of money.

Parliament disagrees with the Stuarts

Trouble had been brewing for a long time between the monarchy and Parliament. Members of Parliament had stopped themselves from complaining out of respect and affection for Queen Elizabeth – but when James arrived they decided to speak their minds. James was used to getting his own way with the Scottish government and was offended by the criticisms of English Members of Parliament.

Elizabeth had been a clever politician who charmed people into doing what she wanted. James lectured and annoyed people. Parliament could not understand why James could no longer survive on his income. They accused James and his court of being extravagant and disliked James' friends, especially George Villiers the Duke of Buckingham (see page 21). When James' son, Charles I (1600-49), came to the throne, Parliament accused his French Catholic Queen, Henriette Marie, of spending too much money.

Charles I with his wife Henriette Marie. The little boy on the left of Charles is the future Charles II.

Words, words, words ....

Many words that we use today meant something different during Stuart times. Some of these boxes will give examples of words whose meanings have changed in the last 300 years.

A water melon was called a 'million' and 'mum' was the name of a German drink.

This Victorian painting shows Charles I trying to arrest five Members of Parliament (see page 8). Charles thought that Parliament was trying to interfere with his Divine Right.

The 'Divine Right of Kings'

Some Members of Parliament wanted more of a say in government. Neither James nor Charles would let this happen. James declared

> *The state of the monarchy is the supremest thing on earth; for kings are not only God's lieutenants* (officers) *on earth, but even by God Himself they are called gods.*
>
> James I in his book, *Basilikon Doron*, written before 1603

James and Charles believed that God had made them kings. James wrote a book, *Basilikon Doron*, about this belief, which was called the Divine Right of Kings.

Charles called three Parliaments in the first years of his reign but they were all disasters. Members of Parliament produced the Petition of Right in 1628 to stop the monarch from raising taxes without consulting them first. In 1629 Parliament condemned the King's actions in the Three Resolutions. Charles was so furious he ruled without Parliament for 11 years.

A soldier, called a musketeer, of James I's time. He had to reload his musket after every shot.

Religion and foreign policy

In 17th-century Europe people took religion very seriously. In England and Wales most people followed the Protestant Anglican Church (the Church of England). The Church of Ireland was also Protestant. In Scotland the church was Presbyterian, a strict form of Protestantism. Puritans were people who were unhappy with the Church of England and Catholics were loyal to the Pope. Catholic countries such as Spain and France were England's enemies.

It's true!

The English mathematician William Oughtred introduced the multiplication symbol 'x' in 1631.

The Civil War and the Commonwealth

War!

Charles I recalled Parliament in 1640 to ask for taxes to be raised. But Members of Parliament wanted to discuss the previous 11 years and complained to him in a document called the Grand Remonstrance (which means the 'big complaint').

In 1642 Charles ordered the arrest of the five leading trouble-makers in Parliament (see page 7), but they escaped. Neither the King nor Parliament would give in and so the Civil War began. The Royalists, who supported the King, were called 'Cavaliers' (a name for a dashing officer), while their opponents were called 'Roundheads' because of their Puritan cropped hairstyles.

Some of Cromwell's New Model Army soldiers.

Cromwell defeats the King

Parliament's General Oliver Cromwell (1599-1658) was a Puritan country gentleman who turned into a brilliant general. He reorganised Parliament's army into a well-trained and equipped force, called the New Model Army. The war ended with the Royalist defeat at the Battle of Naseby in 1645. Charles surrendered to the Scots but they handed him over to Parliament, which tried him for treason (the crime of betraying one's country) and found him guilty.

> None more fond of a king than the English, yet they departed from him to ease their purses and consciences.
>
> Peter Chamberlain, *The Poor Man's Advocate*, 1649

Cromwell fights to rule

Cromwell now had to settle quarrels between Parliament, the army and the supporters of different churches. Parliament began to rule without consulting anyone and spent a great deal of money. Cromwell wanted to execute Charles I but Parliament would not allow this. In 1648 Cromwell sent Colonel Pride and his troops to remove politicians who disagreed with him from the House of Commons. This was called 'Pride's Purge' and the Members of Parliament who were left were called the 'Rump'. Cromwell eventually became just as angry with the Rump and threw them out of the House of Commons as well. Cromwell put his own men into Parliament and they made him Lord Protector and voted to execute the King in 1649.

A portrait of Oliver Cromwell as Lord Protector.

But Cromwell still disliked Parliament so he put Britain under military rule. Britain became a republic (a country without a monarch) called the Commonwealth.

The Irish people still supported the King and in 1650 Cromwell took an army to Ireland to fight rebellions against the Commonwealth. Cromwell ordered the massacre of everyone in the towns of Drogheda and Wexford. People saw that Cromwell was prepared to kill entire towns so the fighting stopped.

In the same year as Cromwell's Irish massacres Charles I's son was crowned Charles II King of Scotland and invaded England with a Scots army. Cromwell beat Charles at Dunbar and at Worcester in 1651. Charles escaped to France after six weeks of adventures that included hiding up an oak tree to avoid capture by Roundheads!

These muskets (at the top) and pistol are the type used by both Cavaliers and Roundheads during the Civil War.

The Restoration

When Cromwell died in 1658 his son Richard took over but he was not as strong a leader as his father. Eighteen months after Cromwell's death General George Monk invited politicians who had been dismissed by Cromwell back to Parliament. These Members of Parliament asked Charles II to return to Britain. Charles II's reign is called the Restoration because the monarchy had been restored to the throne.

The Levellers 1645-49

'The Levellers' were led by John Lilburne and wanted to do away with the monarch, the nobility and all social ranks – hence their name. They wanted every man to have a vote and an elected Parliament to rule the country instead of the King. They also wanted religious freedom (called toleration, see page 10). They set their ideas out in the Agreement of the People in 1647. The Agreement was publicly discussed at a meeting in London and the Levellers gained support. Cromwell, top army officers and wealthy landowners hated these ideas and sent soldiers to stop the Levellers in 1649.

The Declaration of the Levellers of 1649

9

Charles II and James II

Charles II

Charles was welcomed home to scenes of wild rejoicing. Most people had grown sick of Cromwell's Puritan rule which had banned everything from Anglican services, to theatre-going, to maypole dancing! Charles was a kind, witty, clever, easy-going man, who was determined not to 'go on his travels' (be driven into exile) again.

When escaping after the Battle of Worcester (see page 9) Charles II hid from his enemies up an oak tree.

> **H**e has a strange command of himself; he can pass from business to pleasure and from pleasure to business in so easy a manner that all things seem alike to him.
>
> Gilbert Burnet, Bishop of Sailsbury commenting on Charles II

Once back on the throne Charles pardoned almost all of his enemies and tried to allow religious toleration – the right of a person to worship in any way he or she pleased. However, Parliament feared both Catholics and Puritans (now called Nonconformists, see page 15) and so passed a group of acts called the Clarendon Code (1661-5). The Clarendon Code stopped Nonconformists from having important jobs (called public office), made it difficult for them to inherit wealth or to hold meetings and for their priests to travel or teach.

Charles's reign was a very exciting time but it was also filled with disasters such as the Popish Plot (see page 15), the Great Fire (see page 19) and the plague (see page 19).

It's true!

In 1671, Colonel Thomas Blood stole the Crown Jewels. Blood nearly got away with the Jewels, but was captured before it was too late. Charles was so amused he pardoned Blood instead of punishing him.

This painting of 1661 shows Charles II on the way to his coronation. Charles is the tall man on the white horse.

Samuel Pepys

The streets full of nothing but people and horses and carts laden with goods, ready to run over one another, and removing goods from one burned house to another.

The famous diarist Samuel Pepys writing during the Great Fire

Samuel Pepys had an important job as secretary to the Admiralty and wrote his diary between 1660-69. Pepys' diary is one of the most important documents to survive from the Stuart period. Look on pages 17, 21 and 26 for more comments from his diary.

Troubled times

The Dutch were England's greatest rivals in trade, fishing and the race to colonise North America. Two wars were fought against the Dutch from 1665-67 and from 1672-74. England also went to war with France, but Charles preferred to keep on good terms with his cousin, Louis XIV, and even made a treaty with him in 1670.

Charles did not have any children with his wife, Catherine of Braganza, and so his brother James (1633-1701) would inherit the throne. Towards the end of Charles's reign people who were prepared to allow his Catholic brother James to be king were nick-named Tories. Those who wanted to keep James off the throne were called Whigs.

James II

James was not clever or tactful like his brother. He became a Catholic in 1670 and his second wife was a Catholic princess, Mary of Modena. James' religion made him unpopular and he was forced to give up his post of Admiral of the Navy because Catholics and Nonconformists were not allowed to have important government jobs. When James became king his ideas on kingship and religion angered and frightened many of his subjects. After only three years of James' rule Parliament invited his daughter Mary, and her Dutch husband William, Prince of Orange, to rule instead.

James escaped to France and then tried to get his throne back with French soldiers. He invaded Ireland in 1689 but was beaten by William at the Battle of the Boyne (1690). In Scotland the Jacobites (the name for supporters of James II) rebelled but were defeated at the Battle of Dunkeld.

Monmouth's rebellion

Charles II's wife was unable to give him a child, but he had several children outside marriage with his many lovers. He made the eldest of these children the Duke of Monmouth. When Charles died, Monmouth tried to seize the throne but his rebellion collapsed and he was beheaded. Three hundred of his followers were hanged by Judge Jeffreys at the 'Bloody Assizes' and a further 800 were sold as slaves.

A miniature of James Duke of York (later James II) painted in 1661 by Samuel Cooper (see page 26).

 Words, words, words ....

The name 'Tories' was originally given to Irish bandits!

The name 'Whigs' originally referred to Scottish cattle thiefs!

William III, Mary II and Anne

James was defeated in Ireland by William at the Battle of the Boyne (1690, see page 11). The victory of William of Orange is remembered in an Orange Day march every year in Northern Ireland and Scotland. This modern banner showing William is carried in one of the marches.

This blue and white plate shows William and Mary as joint sovereigns.

The Glorious Revolution

Mary II (1662-94) and Anne (1665-1714) were the Protestant daughters of James II and his first wife, Anne Hyde. Mary was asked to rule in her father's place but she insisted on ruling with her Dutch husband, William III (1650-1702), as a joint sovereign.

The events of 1688 were called The Glorious Revolution because people were relieved that the King had been replaced without bloodshed. Parliament made several laws to control the power of the monarch and give Parliament more say in the running of the country. The Declaration of Rights was issued by Parliament in 1689 and Nonconformists were given freedom of worship in the Toleration Act of the same year. The Triennial Act of 1694 made it law for a new Parliament to be elected every three years so no king or queen could rule without Parliament. In 1701 the Act of Settlement made sure that only a Protestant could inherit the throne so religious arguments could be avoided.

William was prepared to agree to any conditions Parliament set, as long as he could declare war on his old enemy, Louis XIV of France. War, known as the War of the League of Augsburg, was declared on France in 1689 and lasted until the Treaty of Ryswick in 1697.

William and the mole

Mary was very popular and people were sad when she died in 1694.

> *It is impossible to describe the desolation which this death has caused the nation.*
>
> The Imperial Ambassador talking about the death of Mary

William continued to rule after Mary's death but people did not like him. William died after his horse stumbled over a mole-hill and threw him. Many people drank to 'the little gentleman in black velvet' who had caused his death.

Anne

A painting of Marlborough's victory at the Battle of Ramillies in 1706.

William and Mary were unable to have children so Mary's sister, Anne, became Queen after William's death. She was married to a Danish prince, George. Anne had 17 pregnancies but all of her children died.

The War of the Spanish Succession (1702-13), which was caused by Louis XIV of France illegally putting his grandson on the Spanish throne, raged throughout Anne's reign. In this war the British general, John Churchill (later created Duke of Marlborough), led allied forces to great victories at the battles of Blenheim, Ramillies, Oudenarde and Malplaquet between 1704 and 1709. These victories turned Britain into a powerful political nation in Europe. But despite the victories, the war became expensive and unpopular and was ended with the Treaty of Utrecht.

After Anne, the next person in direct line to the throne was Sophia, Electress of Hanover, who was related to James I's daughter Elizabeth. Sophia died just before Anne so her son became King George I (1660-1727). The period of rule that George began in 1714 is called Hanoverian.

England and Scotland join

In 1707, after a great deal of bargaining, the Act of Union sealed the political union between England and Scotland. The two countries shared a common Parliament and flag until 1999, when Scotland opened its own parliament in Edinburgh.

Religious life

The Catholics

Despite all the prejudices against them, some people were still faithful to the Roman Catholic Church. There were more Catholics in Ireland than anywhere else, so James I started encouraging Protestants to emigrate to Ireland in 1611.

The Puritans

Charles I and William Laud, Archbishop of Canterbury tried to make Anglican services more beautiful and solemn by using things such as candles, expensive clothes (called vestments) and making the sign of the cross. Some people in the Anglican Church, called Puritans, felt that Charles and Laud were making the Church of England too much like their old enemy, the Catholic Church. The Puritans disagreed with Charles and Laud in Parliament and declared that bishops were not needed.

In Scotland the ideas of Charles and Laud were hated so much that people signed the National Covenant (1638) which said that they would resist any reforms they did not agree with. To gain Scottish support during the English Civil War the English Parliament made the Solemn League and Covenant with the Scots. The Scots sent an army to fight in England and in return their Presbyterian type of worship was introduced into England. During the Commonwealth, Puritan groups were allowed to worship but Cromwell banned Anglican services in 1655.

Words, words, words ....

The word 'cabal' came into use during the reign of Charles II and it now means 'political group'. Charles had a special inner group of five ministers. Their names were Clifford, Arlington, Buckingham, Ashley-Cooper and Lauderdale. People took the initial letters of their names and made the word cabal, using it as a shorthand way of refering to the five ministers.

The Puritans banned many ordinary peoples' favourite pastimes, includng sports. This is a picture of Puritans burning a book about sports on a Sunday. The Puritan crowd are wearing very plain clothes.

It's true!

Every household (including Nonconformist and Catholic households) had to give one tenth of their yearly produce or profits to the Church of England.

The Nonconformists

When Charles II returned, the Church of England was also restored and the lands it had lost under the Commonwealth were given back. Many Puritans decided to leave the Church of England and they became known as Nonconformists or Dissenters. The main dissenting groups were Congregationalists, Presbyterians, Baptists and Quakers.

The Popish Plot and a Catholic king

This so-called plot shows just how frightened ordinary people were of Catholicism. A man called Titus Oates claimed that there was a plot to kill Charles II, put his Catholic brother James on the throne and massacre Protestants. There was no truth in this at all, but people believed him and about 35 innocent Catholics were killed.

When James II became a Roman Catholic in 1670, he became very unpopular. When James became King in 1685, people feared that he would try to force the country to become Catholic.

Titus Oates being punished after his lies about Catholics were exposed

The Gunpowder Plot

A picture from 1606 showing the conspirators of the Gunpowder Plot. The leader, Robert Catesby, is second from the right and Guy Fawkes stands next to him on the left.

After their execution the heads of the traitors were displayed on poles.

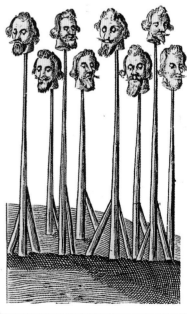

...they shall receive a terrible blow this Parliament and yet they shall not see who hurts them.

The anonymous letter to Lord Monteagle

In 1605 a group of Catholic gentlemen decided to blow up James I and both Houses of Parliament. They wanted to put James's son on the throne and bring him up as a Catholic. But the government was warned by an anonymous letter and Guy Fawkes was found as he was about to light the fuse! The plotters were arrested, tortured and executed.

Life in the countryside

If you could be magically transported back in time to the 17th century you would notice that there were very few people around! There were about five million people in England and Wales, about a million in Scotland and another million in Ireland.

Farming

Most people made their living from farming. In some areas people raised sheep, in others cattle, and for 30 miles around London people grew fruit and vegetables for the city and the court. In some places long strips of land were enclosed to make individual farms but in others, farmers were given strips of land where they grew grain. They kept cattle, sheep and pigs on land that belonged to everyone (called common land). In autumn, most of the animals were killed because there was not enough hay and straw to feed them all winter. By spring, many people's food supplies were running low and much of what was left was mouldy, so people fell ill.

A woodcut of an early 17th-century farmer ploughing a field with oxen

Clothes

In the 17th century fashions changed a great deal but poor people wore clothes that were practical and cheap. To see what rich people wore look at the pictures on pages 6, 7, 10, 20, 21 and 29.

Ordinary working men wore plain baggy shirts, jackets, called doublets, and short trousers, called breeches, made of the roughest linen and wool. Women wore linen shirts under tightly-fitting tops, called bodices. Their wide, full-length skirts were usually made of wool.

Children's clothes were similar to that of adults.

It's true!

During the Stuart period one baby in three died before they reached five and most people died before they were 35 years old.

People dancing around a maypole. The musician is playing a flute and banging a drum.

Change and improvement

In the 17th century there were plenty of new ideas about improving farming and people began to travel between the country and the town more often.

It was so rare for a country gentleman to come to London, that when he did come, he used to make his will before he set out.

Samuel Pepys, 1669

New crops like potatoes and turnips were introduced, but were not popular. Growing new crops meant that you did not have to leave a field fallow (unused) once every three years to let it recover its goodness. The new crops could also be used to feed animals during the winter, so fewer animals had to be killed in the autumn. If more animals survived then more manure was available to enrich the soil, so harvests were larger. However, most small farmers resisted these improvements because they were usually suggested by more powerful landowners who wanted to enclose the common land the smaller farmer needed. But new crops were grown and by the second half of the century, starvation was rarer than ever before.

Country people at play

Life was very hard so people took every chance they could to enjoy themselves. They celebrated weddings, christenings, Christmas, Whitsun, harvest, sheepshearing, Lammas, May Day and Michaelmas. These festivals were an excuse for music, singing, dancing, drinking and feasting. There were fairs, wrestling contests and horse races. Games like ninepins (skittles) and an early version of football were played. They also enjoyed cruel 'sports' like cock fighting and bear baiting.

Witches

People in the British Isles believed that witches existed. James I thought that witches were real and wrote a book about them called *Daemonologie*.

Most people who were accused of witchcraft were disliked by their neighbours – perhaps because they looked odd, or said nasty things about people. When something awful happened – a baby died or the cattle became sick – people looked for someone to blame. People accused of witchcraft might be tortured and, if found guilty, were hung.

In 1645-47 Matthew Hopkins, the so-called Witch-finder General, toured Essex and its neighbouring counties. He executed several hundred people as witches. The last execution for witchcraft in England took place in 1712.

A picture from 1612 showing witches riding on a pig

Life in towns

Three new drinks were introduced in the 17th century – coffee, tea and hot chocolate – but they were too expensive for many people. The first coffee shop opened in Oxford in 1650. This is a London coffee house of 1668.

There were very few towns and cities in the 17th century and they were very small by our standards. London had about 500,000 people living in it by 1700. Only Birmingham, Bristol, Exeter, Newcastle, Norwich and York had more than 10,000 inhabitants and only 23 towns had more than 5,000 people living in them.

Smells and pollution

Most town houses were made of wood and plaster. Houses were often packed together along very narrow streets. Homes did not usually have a water supply and waste was thrown into the street where dogs, cats and rats fought over it until it rotted. Cities were very noisy and smelt awful. Air pollution was a problem in London. John Evelyn complained of....

Horrid smoke, which obscures our churches and makes our palaces look old, which fouls our clothes and corrupts the waters....

Flies, fleas and lice

Living conditions in towns were so bad that disease spread easily. Dirt, flies, fleas and lice were a normal part of many peoples' lives. People did not know about germs and many of them hardly ever washed. When they were sick, the rich could call a physician (a doctor), from the Royal College of Physicians. But there weren't many physicians and they did not really know much about disease. Blood-letting (using leeches to suck blood out of people) was their standard remedy. An operation was practically a death sentence because without anaesthetics the shock of the pain was likely to kill any patient. Even if patients survived the operation, infection, caused by the dirty conditions, was likely to kill them.

In towns you might turn to an apothecary (someone rather like a modern-day chemist) for a medicine, but apothecaries were expensive. Many people relied on herbal medicines made at home. Every wealthy lady had a stock of plant medicines to treat her family

It's true!

The first postal service appeared in London in 1680.

The first street lamps were lit in London in 1680 and were fuelled with oil.

Carts full of dead to bury.

and servants. In both town and country, certain men and women became known for their skill at mixing medicines and making charms to protect their patients from disease.

Bring out your dead!

The plague first appeared in Europe in the mid-14th century. The plague was carried by fleas that lived on black rats. When a flea bit someone they would be infected. There was no known cure and few people who caught the plague survived.

From 1665-66 about 100,000 people died of the 'black death' in Britain. Death carts went through the streets for weeks. The men driving the carts shouted 'bring out your dead' and people would hand over the bodies of those who had died so that they could be buried. Plague victims were buried in massive pits because there were too many of them for individual graves to be dug.

Hundreds of people left London to escape the plague. You can see the three spires of the medieval Saint Paul's Cathedral in the background.

Words, words, words ....

A room with a bath in it was called a hot-house and a toilet was called a house of office.

Fire!

Fire was feared in the countryside but in towns it could be a terrible disaster. There were no organised fire brigades, though some town councils kept a few buckets handy as well as iron hooks for pulling burning buildings down. As there was no insurance against fire, families could lose their homes and possessions and be left with nothing.

The worst and most famous fire of all was the great fire of London which raged for four days in September 1666. It was started by a careless apprentice in a baker's shop in Pudding Lane. It destroyed about four-fifths of the city. About 13,000 houses were destroyed, 87 parish churches, the great medieval cathedral of Saint Paul's and many public buildings like the Guildhall. About 130,000 people were left homeless. The fire did have one good result – though people did not realise it at the time – it killed most of the rats and so helped to get rid of the plague.

A picture of London burning, painted in 1666.

Life at court

Charles II's royal gardener presents him with a pineapple. Pineapples had only just been brought to Britain.

A hand-embroidered jacket from the reign of James I.

The monarch had several palaces in and around London (but not Buckingham Palace which was not bought until much later). Kings and queens sometimes travelled around their kingdom to see the state of the realm for themselves. It was important for the monarch to be seen by his or her subjects as, without television and radio, people needed to be reassured that the monarch was still alive. Wherever the monarch went, the court also went. The court was made up of hundreds of people, from dukes to humble servants and it was the centre of the political, social and artistic life of the day.

The court provided the rich and gorgeous setting for the monarch and the monarch's family. The royal family led a lot of their lives in public. They often dined in public and ordinary people pressed into the Banqueting Hall to watch them.

Ambassadors and spies

The court was the centre of power because the monarch ruled the country and appointed ministers and officials to carry out his or her plans and decisions. The monarch held regular meetings with his ministers, called Privy Council meetings, where every aspect of government was discussed – from justice and taxation to trade, industry, foreign policy and war. There were always ministers, officials and foreign ambassadors waiting to see the monarch and spies reporting back with their information.

Anyone who wanted power, money and a job, called an office, travelled to the court. They would try to win favour with the monarch, a member of the royal family, or one of the monarch's particular friends in order to be appointed to a position.

Favourites

A male or female courtier (member of the court) who was a close friend of the monarch was called a 'favourite'. A favourite could become rich and powerful but often made enemies. George Villiers was James I's favourite. He won fame, fortune, power and a title (Duke of Buckingham) and managed to keep it all under Charles I. But he was eventually stabbed to death by a servant.

A portrait of George, first Duke of Buckingham.

Jokes, gambling and art

The behaviour of the court was decided by the monarch. James I enjoyed rude jokes and drunken parties, while Charles I enjoyed art and music. There were magnificent ceremonies, parties and entertainments. Under the first two Stuarts, masques (musical plays) were popular and members of the royal family took part in them. Charles II loved dancing and the theatre and was a regular visitor to London's Theatre Royal in Drury Lane.

> *When the King dances, all the ladies in the room, and the Queen herself, stands up; and indeed he dances rarely* (well) *and much better than the Duke of York.*
>
> Samuel Pepys writing in his diary about a royal ball attended by Charles II

The court was also a centre of learning, art and good taste. Composers, poets, musicians, painters and entertainers all needed wealthy people (called patrons) to employ them and so made their way to the court. Authors, mathematicians, astronomers and scientists also flocked to the court in order to gain the attention of the monarch (see pages 26-29).

It's true!

Charles I bought the Duke of Mantua's amazing art treasures for £25,000 and so collected the greatest art collection ever owned by a single monarch. Unfortunately, most of this collection was sold off during the Commonwealth.

Charles II watches a horse race at Windsor Castle, 1684.

Words, words, words ....

Wine was called 'wind' during Stuart times. Spanish red wine was called 'tent'.

Exploration and empire

By 1600 the outline of the Americas or 'New World' was known. The Spaniards controlled Latin America so English explorers like Henry Hudson concentrated on finding a northwest passage (route) to China. Hudson led four expeditions. On the last in 1610 he found the bay named after him but died when his men mutinied (rebelled) and sent him and his son out to sea in an open boat. In 1616 William Baffin got to northeast Canada and discovered the bay and island that are named after him. Hudson's Bay gave the British a way to reach the rich fur trade in Canada without having to go through French-held lands.

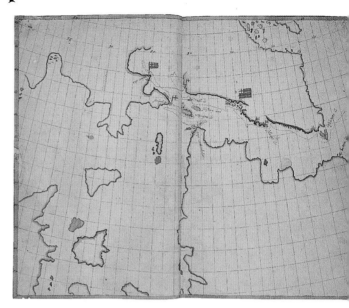

William Baffin's chart of his voyage of 1615.

A replica of the *Mayflower*

The Quaker William Penn gave gifts to the Indians as part of the treaty he made with them to safeguard his colony in Pennsylvania.

The wild west – 17th century style

The first permanent English colony in North America was set up at Jamestown in 1607. These pioneers were followed by people who hoped to find religious freedom in the New World. In 1620 the *Mayflower* sailed with Puritan settlers – the Pilgrim Fathers – and in 1632 Maryland was founded for Catholic settlers. Other colonies followed, such as South Carolina in 1670 and Pennsylvania, settled by the Quaker William Penn and a group of his followers in 1681.

The Dutch also had colonies in America. After a war between Britain and Holland, the defeated Dutch had to give their town of New Amsterdam to the British. It was renamed New York, after Charles II's brother James, Duke of York.

Words, words, words ....

A 'mould' was the Stuart name for a full-scale wooden pattern, or pieces of a ship, that was made before the ship was built.

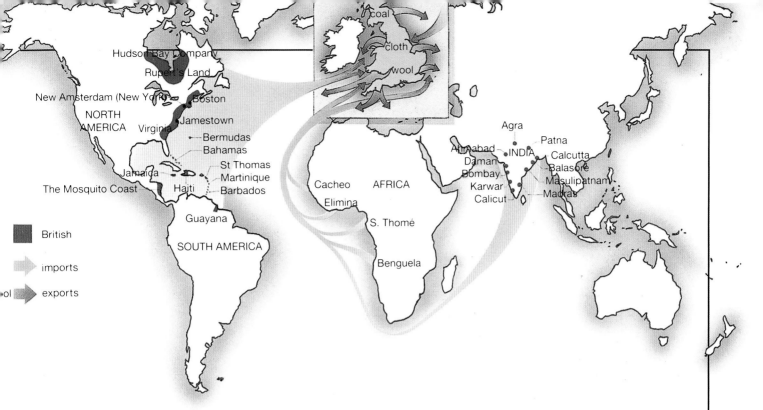

A map of the world showing some British colonies and trade during the Stuart period.

Empire building

Dutch merchants forced the English East India Company out of the East Indies so the Company set up in India. The British Empire in India grew from the Company's small trading stations. This increase in overseas colonies and trade made Charles II set up a special committee of the Privy Council to specialise in colonial affairs.

In 1704, during the War of the Spanish Succession (see page 13), Britain captured the Rock of Gibraltar from Spain. In the final peace treaty Britain kept Gibraltar and was given the right to supply the Spanish American colonies with African slaves (see page 24).

Buccaneers!

Britain and France constantly attacked Spanish ships in the waters of the West Indies – with the help of buccaneers. Buccaneers should not be confused with pirates. Pirates attacked ships of all nations, including their own. A buccaneer was the captain of a private merchant ship, who carried a letter from his sovereign, allowing him to attack enemy ships. In the 16th century Francis Drake and Walter Raleigh attacked Spanish ships and were regarded as heroes by the English, but the Spaniards thought they were pirates.

Buccaneers attacked Spanish galleons returning from Latin America laden with gold. Buccaneers also helped to capture some West Indian islands from Spain and set up a fortified (well defended) base on the island of Tortuga. When William III made peace with Spain some buccaneers returned to being ordinary merchants, but many chose to become real pirates. They crossed the Atlantic Ocean, set up a base on the island of Madagascar, and attacked ships returning from the Far East with fabulously rich cargoes.

It's true!

Being a colonist in America was difficult and dangerous. Of the 104 men and boys who went to Virginia in 1607, 51 were dead by the following spring. Of the 102 pilgrims on the *Mayflower*, 40 died during the first winter.

Trade and industry

London controlled most of England's foreign trade handling about seven-eighths of all imports (goods brought into the country) and exports (goods sold to other countries). The Scots traded very profitably with North Germany, Poland and the Baltic.

The British fought the Dutch over trade three times during the 17th century. These Dutch ships are trading spices in the Far East in the 1640s.

Trading wars

The Dutch were Europe's most successful traders but British merchants were determined to overtake them.

> *What we want is more of the trade the Dutch now have.*
>
> The Duke of Albemarle, 1662

In 1651 Parliament passed the Navigation Act, a new law which said that all goods brought into Britain had to be carried in British ships, or the ships of the country the goods came from. This helped British shipping, but led to wars with the Dutch who were now unable to do as much trade with Britain. By the second half of the century, British trading companies were more successful than ever before.

Tea and slavery

In 1644 the Manchu Dynasty came to power in China and allowed trade with the West (China did not really trade with the West before this time). Tea started to be imported into Britain. It was fashionable to drink tea with sugar and so British colonies in the West Indies and the southern states of North America began growing sugar. They used African slaves to do the work and made huge profits. British merchants took goods, such as knives and swords, to West Africa and exchanged them for men, women and children. The slaves were taken to America and exchanged for sugar, tobacco and later, cotton. Liverpool and Bristol were important ports by the end of the century because they controlled most of the slave trade.

It's true!

Abram Darby began using coke and coal to smelt iron in 1709.

Thomas Savery invented a steam pump in 1698.

Thomas Newcomen invented a steam engine in 1712.

The Bank of England was founded in 1694.

Cloth, coal and iron

Woollen cloth was England's most important industry and export. Scotland also produced woollen cloth, Wales specialised in flannel and Ireland in linen. Rich merchants called clothiers bought wool and hired country people to do the spinning and weaving. This work was usually done at home and so it became known as a cottage industry. The cloth was then collected and taken to be made into clothes.

Tin, lead, copper, zinc and silver were all mined, but coal was the most important mining industry. Miners (men, women and children) worked in terrible conditions with only candles for light, which sometimes caused fatal fires. Coal miners were regarded as outcasts by other people, who would not marry them because they thought they would bring bad luck. When extra labour was needed criminals and beggars were forced to work in the pits. But coal mining was a fast-growing industry because coal was used for heating and cooking.

Most iron was made in Sussex and the Midlands where there were large supplies of iron ore and wood. After the iron ore had been dug out of the ground it was heated in a fire so that the pure metal could be taken out of it — this is called smelting.

A 17th-century weaver at his loom.

Transport

Seventeenth-century roads were usually bad because they did not have good, hard surfaces. Heavy goods were taken by carriers' carts. Poor people sometimes hitched rides on carriers' carts, but usually had to walk. The rich travelled on horseback or in coaches. Travelling could be dangerous with highwaymen lying in wait to rob travellers.

Heavy goods were transported by boat. Barges travelled along rivers, while the coasts hundreds of small ships carried goods from port to port. There were 300 boats just for carrying coal from Newcastle to London. Coastal shipping faced danger from storms and 'wreckers', people who used lights to lure ships to destruction on rocks during storms in order to steal their cargoes.

Highwaymen in action

Words, words, words ....

A trading station was called a 'factory'. Later this word changed to mean the name of a place where things are made rather than a place where things are sold.

The arts

A portrait of Shakespeare from an edition of his plays printed in 1623.

A play being performed at the Red Bull Playhouse in London in 1672. The rich people sit in the gallery and the rest of the audience sit around the stage.

In the 17th century art and literature were influenced by the cultures of ancient Greece and Rome that had been rediscovered during the Renaissance (see Words, words, words ....).

Theatre

Shakespeare (1564-1616) wrote and produced some of his 38 plays – *Hamlet, Othello, King Lear, Macbeth* and *The Tempest* at the Globe Theatre in London during the reign of James I. At this time, all the female roles in plays were acted by boys. In the reign of Charles I a French theatre company came to London with actresses and people were so outraged that there was a riot. In those days theatres and theatre audiences were very different to today. The Globe was partly open-air with a thatched (later tiled) roof over the stage. People paid three pence to sit in a seat in one of the three galleries arranged around the stage. For two pence you could stand in one of the galleries and a penny let you sit on the ground. Seventeenth-century theatre-goers were very rude and talked, shouted, ate, distracted the actors and walked about during the performance.

Theatres were closed during the Commonwealth but re-opened after the Restoration. The Theatre Royal, Drury Lane, was the most successful Restoration theatre. Actressess now played women's parts and one of the most famous was one of Charles II's lovers, Nell Gwynne, an orange seller turned actress who specialised in comedy roles. After the Restoration comedies about polite society poked fun at fashions, wealthy people and their behaviour.

The stage is now a thousand times better and more glorious than before... Now, all things civil, no rudeness anywhere; then, as in a bear-garden (mad house). *Then two or three fiddlers; now, nine or ten of the best.*

Samuel Pepys commenting in his diary (1667)
on the difference between the theatre before and after the Civil War

Art

Miniature portraits were fashionable. John Hoskins painted Charles I and Samuel Cooper painted Oliver Cromwell, Charles II and James II (see page 11). The Stuarts hired three great Dutch artists to work for them – Peter Paul Rubens, Anthony van Dyck and Peter Lely.

Words, words, words ....

The name Renaissance means re-birth in French and it refers to the 're-birth' of interest in the ancient arts of Greece and Rome in 14th–16th-century Europe. The Renaissance inspired people to investigate many different areas of life, such as music, politics, literature, medicine and art.

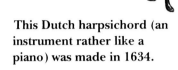

Peter Paul Rubens came to England as a diplomat but stayed to decorate the Banqueting Hall of Whitehall in London. Both Anthony van Dyck and Peter Lely settled and worked in England, painting wonderful portraits of the royal family and the nobility. Painters had to be diplomats and paint people in a flattering way. It is said that Peter Lely painted Mary and Anne's ladies in waiting with their mouths closed because they all ate so much sugar that their teeth were either black or had fallen out completely.

This Dutch harpsichord (an instrument rather like a piano) was made in 1634.

Architecture

Inigo Jones, Christopher Wren and John Vanburgh were the greatest architects of the 17th century. Inigo Jones was inspired by Greek and Roman architecture and the 16th-century Italian architect Andrea Palladio. Jones was very talented and designed theatre sets and costumes as well as houses. He designed the Banqueting Hall in Whitehall and the Queen's House at Greenwich.

Christopher Wren is famous for the 51 churches he built after the fire of London (including Saint Paul's Cathedral), but he also designed university colleges, palaces and houses.

At the end of the century John Vanbrugh (who also wrote plays) designed grand buildings such as Castle Howard and Blenheim Palace. Blenheim Palace was built for John Churchill, Duke of Marlborough, as a reward for his battle victories (see page 13).

Brilliant writers

Many writers were at work during the Stuart period – some of the most important ones are listed below.

John Donne (1572-1631), a parson and poet who wrote beautiful love poems.

John Milton (1608-74), a Puritan poet whose most famous work is *Paradise Lost* (1667).

John Bunyan (1628-88), a Puritan writer, author of the *Pilgrim's Progress*.

Jonathan Swift (1667-1745), an author whose most famous work, *Gullivers' Travels*, was published in George I's time.

Blenheim Palace

Science and medicine

The Renaissance not only had a great influence on art, architecture and literature, it also made people ask questions in all areas of life. People became more interested in science and tried to find out how the natural world worked. During the 17th century, people began to classify, or describe, plants and animals. In his *General Account of Plants*, written between 1686 and 1704, John Ray (1627-1705) described over 17,000 plants. John Ray divided his plants up into different classes depending on the shape of their leaves and the kind of fruit they produced. He was the first person to see that plants were made up of many tiny cells.

During the Stuart reign it became very fashionable for wealthy people to collect, catalogue and commission drawings of plants and animals. This book of plants was commissioned by the Duchess of Beaufort in 1703. The picture is of a milkwort plant.

A portrait of Isaac Newton painted in 1703, the year he became President of the Royal Society.

The great scientists

Sir Francis Bacon wrote some very important books on science. He told people to collect facts, do experiments and make careful notes on everything they saw. He thought that scientists should try to improve the quality of everyone's lives. His books inspired many 17th-century scientists.

Exciting discoveries by European scholars like Galileo (1564-1642) were eagerly studied in Britain. Charles II was very interested in science and gave the Royal Society a charter in 1662. Even today, membership of the Royal Society is one of the highest honours in the scientific world.

Isaac Newton (1642-1727) is one of the world's most famous scientists. He was a professor of mathematics at Cambridge University. In his great work, known as the *Principia*, he explains his discovery of gravity, the force that pulls things to the Earth. His ideas were inspired by watching an apple fall from a tree. He went on to show that gravity was the force that pulled the planets around the sun. Another of his great discoveries, published in *Opticks*, points out that

sunlight is made up of a mixture of the colours of the spectrum – red, orange, yellow, green, blue, indigo and violet.

In 1628 the Royal Physician, William Harvey (1578-1657), published his discoveries about how blood moves around the body (circulation). Harvey's work was a great step forward in understanding how the human body works.

Inventions

Robert Hooke (1635-1703) was a scientist with wide interests. One of his great achievements was the invention of the balance spring used to power watches. He also wrote an important book called *Micrographia*, which illustrated some of the specimens he had examined, and the microscopes and other instruments he had designed. Together with Robert Boyle (1627-91) he designed and built a special pump that created a vacuum (a place without air) by pumping air out of a glass globe. This enabled people to do experiments on air pressure and to study how plants and animals breathe.

A picture of William Harvey explaining his theory about the movement of blood around the body to Charles I.

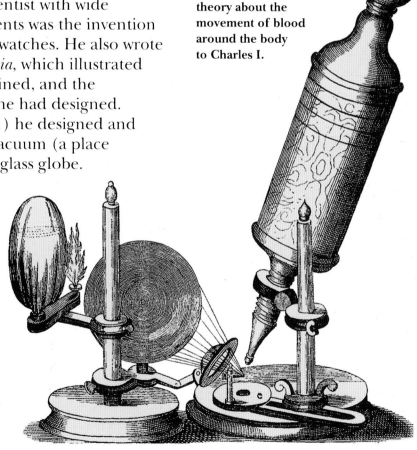

This is a drawing of the microscope made by Robert Hooke in 1662. The main part of the microscope is on the right-hand side. The complicated instrument on the left-hand side provides white light for the scientist to examine the specimen under.

Index

Glossary

abdicate to leave the throne
Admiralty the office of the commander of the Navy
allies people or countries who agree to support each other
ambassador someone who is a representative of his or her country in a foreign land
anaesthetics substances that cause people to become numb wherever the substance is injected (local anaesthetic). A person becomes completely unconscious when under a general anaesthetic
anonymous by a person whose name is unknown
Banqueting Hall a grand hall in Whitehall started in the time of James I
bear baiting a 17th-century entertainment which involved dogs attacking chained-up bears. Bear baiting is now illegal
charter a document issued by a king or queen to a company which states how and what it can trade or do
cock fighting a fight between two cocks that have sharp metal spikes fixed around their legs. Cock fighting is now illegal
colonise to settle in a foreign land. Sometimes people were sent to colonise a country as a punishment
dynasty the name for a series of rulers who inherit power
English East India Company a company founded in 1600 to trade with the East Indies. Because the Dutch dominated trade in this area the Company set up in India. The British government took over the running of India from the Company in 1874
Evelyn, John (1620-1706) an English diarist and author
Far East the countries of East Asia eg: China, Japan and Malaysia
Galileo an Italian mathematician, astronomer and scientist. Galileo perfected the telescope and watched the stars in great detail
Lammas the feast day of 1 August, held to celebrate Saint Peter's escape from prison
massacre to kill large numbers of people at the same time
Michaelmas the feast day of Saint Michael which takes place on 29 September
monarchy the royal family
realm kingdom
Pope the leader of the Catholic Church on earth
scholar someone who is an expert in a particular subject.
sovereign king or queen
spectrum the colours that can be seen when light is split into the colours of the rainbow as it passes through a prism. A prism is a piece of glass with triangular ends and a rectangular middle
Whitsun the feast day of 15 May

Places to visit

Many wonderful houses and collections have survived from the Stuart period. There are also houses built earlier which contain many Stuart items. Local museums may also have information and objects from the Civil War and daily life in Stuart Britain.

Avon (near Bristol) – Dryham Park
Cambridgeshire (Ely) – Oliver Cromwell's House
Cornwall – Godolphin House
Derbyshire – Bolsover Castle
Dorset – Chettle House, Corfe Castle, Kingston Lacy House
Essex – Audley End House
Gloucestershire – Little Dean Hall
Hampshire – Basing House
Hertfordshire – Hatfield House, Cromer Windmill
Isle of Wight – Carisbrooke Castle, Nunwell House
Kent – Squerryes Court
Leicestershire – Belgrave Hall, Stanford Hall
Lincolnshire – Belton House, Woolsthorpe Manor
London – Fenton House, Ham House, Kensington Palace, the Monument, Museum of Garden History, Museum of London, Saint Paul's Cathedral
Greenwich – the Old Royal Observatory, the Queen's House,
Middlesex – Hampton Court Palace
Northamptonshire – Cottesbrooke Hall, Holdenby House, Thrumpton Hall
Oxfordshire – Blenheim Palace, Broughton Castle, Kingston Bagpuize House, Rousham House
Shropshire – Boscobel House
Staffordshire – Moseley Old Hall
Suffolk – Otley Hall
Sussex – Petworth House
Warwickshire – Ragley Hall
West Midlands – Aston Hall
Wiltshire – Wilton House
Yorkshire – Treasurer's House, East Riddlesden
Wales – Erddig
Northern Ireland – Springhill
Culross (Scotland) – The Town House and Study
Edinburgh – Gladstone's Land